Betrayal Creek

Betrayal Creek

W. K. Stratton

LITERARY PRESS
LAMAR UNIVERSITY

ISBN: 978-1-942956-81-5
Library of Congress Control Number: 2020943844

Manufactured in the USA

Lamar University Literary Press
Beaumont, Texas

I came to explore the wreck.
The words are purposes.
The words are maps.
I came to see the damage that was done
and the treasures that prevail.

—Adrienne Rich

For my money, our true poets begin
their poems in the place "past
weeping" …sometimes fuming,
sometimes singing and dancing …
[and] we are able to see a ruin we
hardly knew was there.

—Gerald Stern

I'm a Westerner and
not afraid
of my shadow.

—Diane Wakoski

To Charles Plymell and Roxie Powell
And to the memory of Chuck Kinder

CONTENTS

Introduction

I wrote the poems in this collection after I finished work on my book, *The Wild Bunch: Sam Peckinpah, a Revolution in Hollywood, and the Making of a Legendary Film*, in late 2018. Many of these poems were written at airports, on airplanes, and in hotel and motel rooms around the West as I was touring to support the book. It became a critically applauded bestseller; it was certainly the best and most successful nonfiction book I've written. I thought I was on a roll. Many things seemed to be coming together for me on a lot of levels, both professionally and personally.

But that old song's warnings about riding high in April and then being shot down in May proved true. It happened to me. I've had much thrown my way. In several of these poems I refer to the smartest person I know, a woman I consider to be a lifesaver. Six months ago, she said that I have more moving parts to deal with in my life than most people ever have to confront. She was and is right.

Then things became even more complicated and worse. Betrayal is never easy to manage. But here I am. I've never been very good at thriving, but I'm an expert at surviving. Now I just want to find some peace. *Betrayal Creek* was going to be a whole other kind of book with a different title. Life forged it into what it is. Maybe that's a good thing. It is volume four of a larger work I call the *Dreaming Sam Peckinpah Quintet*. The first three volumes are *Dreaming Sam Peckinpah* (2011), *Ranchero Ford/Dying in Red Dirt Country* (2015), and *Colo—State—Pen: 18456* (2018). I've dedicated this book to Charles Plymell and Roxie Powell and to the memory of Chuck Kinder because Charley and Rox have been and continue to be, and Chuck was while he was living, supporters of my poetry and me. I feel indebted to all three for their generosity and friendship.

WKS

May 2020

Near Brushy Creek,
Where people have lived
Continually for around
Fifteen thousand years

Old Westerns

She tells you she wants to end things
Because she hates boxing, Peckinpah
Old cowboy movies, and rodeo —
Where does rodeo come from?
You haven't given it a thought
In more than twelve years.
Never mind.
She demands conclusion.
You watch a Joan Didion documentary
On Netflix at Betrayal Creek.
You both drink and smoke weed.

This final shootout involves no bullets,
Just pity and regret.
Betrayal Creek's woman does not hate you.
You cannot say if you hate her.
But you never want to see Tucson again.
Nor do you want to see River Walk lights
At Christmas.
She possesses an old lover retrieved.
You are forsaken.
Kids outside shoot fireworks
At New Year's midnight
As Didion's neurosis bleeds the screen.
At least Didion understood loving
John Wayne.
This night you love everyone and no one.
You are an ordinary man
With spurs and a saddle-scarred soul.

Betrayal Creek

After she chucked you aside,
You listened to Emmylou and Ronstadt's
Western Wall seventeen times in a row.
It was over a Sunday.
Rain and thunder made nothing better.
She named her house for a creek
That never existed.
That should have been a signal.
You ignored it.
Everything then flowed through you:
Anger, resentment, too much tequila.
This is how romance crashes.
Now you look out a window
At a full moon muddled by low clouds.
Debility is leafless trees and dun grass.

El Patio

The waiters hustle orders
Served with saltines and salsa.
You first came here in 1975.
You like it because it is an old boot.
You like it because she hated it.
El Patio was never in fashion.
Now a mess of queso, arroz, frijoles
Bubbles on el plato before you.
You roll a tortilla de maiz
Until it is an ink pen cylinder
And begin to eat.
El Patio is everything you are
And everything you ever will be.

Seventy Yards Distant

This trip you drink Pacifico beer
And Maxwell House coffee.
You reject her tricked-up cocktails
And designer beans from Ethiopia.
You feel at ease in Gulf fog,
Hydrozoans at your feet.
You rejoice in her being
Three hundred miles removed.

Later you joust octogenarian
Ornithologists with camera lenses
The length of your forearm
To obtain uncluttered vision.
In reeds seventy yards distant
Stand two whooping cranes,
Refugees from wildlife preservation.
You cannot know if they will survive.
But you are at one with these birds
In sour estuary air. This is romance:
The only love that can be trusted.

Lone Wolf

Gird yourself with iron again.
Raise up a turret of granite.
Embrace the lone wolf once more.
You tried the other route
And wound up gelded
By betrayal.

Protect yourself:
Bare your teeth,
Rehearse growl
And glower.
Survive.

Fallen Scaffolding

Rain fell and you listened to "Villanova Junction"
Over and over in a white room
When the last support collapsed.

To her, empathy was diet soda and clever cartoons
Snipped from Sunday papers.

Your license became her exit plan
From recycle bins and responsibility.

You at last fled that twisted scaffold.

In scrubbed light now you read
From Hart Crane's *White Buildings*.

Kisses/granting/worth. . .
Yes. They must be. Someplace.

Tao of Betrayal Creek

The Betrayal Creek that can be stated
Is not the eternal Betrayal Creek.
Betrayal Creek is the origin
Of suffering and disgust.
It is also the offspring
Of earth, heaven, hell, and the universe.
Addicts and scholars attempt definition.
It is foolhardy.
Sobriety and lust:
Two ends of the same rope.
Mystery yanks on itself.
All is one:
Beethoven's 9th symphony/belch
Sistine Chapel/sewage treatment plant
Mona Lisa/iodine on a wound
Caviar/scabies
Mother Teresa/Charles Manson
The Mahatma/Hells Angels
Descartes/bowel movement
Heaven is here on this planet now.
Hell, likewise.

Words Read on the Other Side of the Border Wall

(for Chuy Hernández, April, 2019)

You are a boxer.
The gym is your refuge.
It is your cathedral.
You have stepped into the ring
With people from every corner.
Boxers are brothers and sisters.
With each sparring round
You restate Suzuki:
>   We are not one,
>   We are not not one.

Through headgear
And the canyon
Between your gloves
You study eyes of other men,
Eyes that are also your own,
Eyes everyone possesses.
You respect the common trinity,
Jab, right cross, hook:
>   We are not one,
>   We are not not one.

You have sparred fighters
From Venezuela, Iowa,
Finland, and Peru,
California, Nigeria, Poland,
Canada, Ecuador, Argentina,
Spain, the UK, and China,
New Zealand, Korea, Palestine,
Texas, Mexico, and more:
>   We are not one,
>   We are not not one.

The eyes differ,
The eyes are the same.
There is no distinguishing plasma
Crusted on ancient towels.
Boxing and love
Require boundaries:
No hitting below the belt,
No punches after the bell,
No broken promises,
No elbows in the dark,
Respect, always respect.

So boundaries, yes,
But no sealed borders,
No fences, no walls.
Boxing is your religion.
Love is your blood.

In Brush Country

Nothing is painless here.
Even rattlesnakes suffer
In this mesquite.
Good jobs come from
Drilling and fracking.
And injury to earth and flesh
Abounds — the ancient sorrow.
You move through diesel showers
At the truck stop near Three Rivers
Then buy a Buffalo Outdoors brand
Rig driver work jacket.
It becomes your holy vestment:
With reinforced elbows it is
Ideal for welding and prayer.
Holier now than you ever were
At Betrayal Creek,
You step out into Interstate wind.
You are reclaimed and authentic.

Where the West Finally Dies

Your first mistake:
When sighs and vacant eyes
Began to greet you across tables
In Manchaca dives, you exhaled
As if everything were solid as an
Interstate overpass. For the first time
You stood completely ungirded,
Misinterpreting the sum,
And wound up splintered.
All those years ago
Dylan edged ahead
At Malibu's Shangri-La,
Where the West finally dies.
Dylan hitchhiked the PCH.
Or sometimes he drove a rusty truck.
He slept in a tent or on the grass
Outside the compound
And bedded dozens of women
As he attempted to char his Sara loss.
He wrote a song called "Sign Language."
You knew it well but never absorbed it
Until now.
Today you are in L.A. at your own small café.
Within your skull you stream Link Wray.
You hold a sandwich. It's a quarter to three.
Time never rolls forward from this point.
Up on the PCH was a clam house Peckinpah
Used to frequent. Dylan played piano there.
You were invited but never made it.
Instead you ended up at Betrayal Creek.

Luzita

I.

Holiday season dismal night —
Aren't they all? —
And you find yourself dining
At a glass/stone/asphalt fashion zone.
She raves about the savorless food.
It is a soulless joint
Filled with hollow white people.
But at least the tequila is decent.
She chatters boundlessly.
Then you both walk to your car.
Through the Austin-tepid winter night
You begin the drive to Betrayal Creek.
Narciso Martínez's "Luzita" fills
The dead air between you.
That song is shit, she blurts. I hate it.
What? How can that be?
She then unfurls bolts of duplicity.
She says nothing about you charms her
And exposes her bleached soul of lead.

II.

"Luzita" — how can she scorn it?
Maybe an unchallenged white woman
With Midwest foundation lacks capacity
To embrace the glory
Of Guadalupe and Concepción Rodriguez's
Fiftieth wedding anniversary
On a spring night in Brownsville.
You recall that noble couple
Entering the wood-paneled hall
Beneath a flowered arch
To applause and conjunto —
Narciso's fingers flying the buttons
Of his red accordion.
It is lost on her.
She'd prefer a dead Beatles tune.
Or the narcissistic whimpers
Of washed out singer-songwriters
At trendy venues downtown.

III.

You understand what is coming.
She's returning to the scientist
Who is a decade her junior,
Who resembles nothing so much
As a euthanized praying mantis,
A grownup who frolics with
pretend epees
And obsesses over *Game of Thrones*.
Jesus —
With tequila eloquence
You express your outrage
Over dishonor and deceit
And complete disrespect.
You did everything right this time.
These are her words.
You did everything right. . .
Eventually you both climb
Into her worn-out bed
And soon her alcoholic snoring
Thunders walls
In this dreadful dwelling.
You can't sleep. You want out.

Only highways have loved you.
That is how it will always be.
You play Narciso Martínez
In your mind: "Luzita"
Now and always.

Sam Peckinpah Pulled

Sam Peckinpah pulled
A book from you
In the midst of woe.
Each keystroke was
A heart attack.
You never suffered more.
Sam stood in your room
Calling you a dumb fuck,
A lazy shit-head.
He'd been dead
Thirty-three years.
You never met him
Yet he spoke to you.
Every single day
You lit a San Judas Tadeo
Veladora on your desk —
Patron saint of lost causes,
Patron saint of W.K. Stratton,
And by holy candlelight flicker
You pushed ahead
As dawn broke.

The Leon

I.

You lived along the Leon River in Belton.
Sometimes you smelled flood water
From your back porch.
Once a great horned owl flew past low,
A full-grown cat in its talons.
A year later, a heron of some sort
Built a nest in the woods:
A five-gallon bucket of sticks and mud.
Someone murdered the owner of a café
A few blocks down the street.
Six shots to the head at midnight:
No money went missing.
You knew the crime would go unsolved.
You had lived in Texas forever.
Your wife moved to a different bedroom.
You did not care.

II.

You'd drive to a beer joint called He's Not Here
And listen to the Georges on the jukebox,
Strait and Jones.
You played golf on the municipal course
That hugged the river. You paid green fees
To an old drunk who wore overalls.
A blind dog sat on his lap.
You never really cured your shank.
One January morning your mother called
To say your brother was dead in Fort Worth.
You couldn't tell if she was crying.
The Leon was little more than a creek
        that season.
A hundred bluebirds and more
Descended on winterkill grass
Just as you hung up.
You took a six-pack of Pearl
Down to the river for last rites.

Pandemic Romance

This woman is complete and undisguised.
Your acquaintance rolls back for decades.
But counters always separated you.
Now social distancing divides you more.
You ask for pastrami. You are 1747 miles
From Second Avenue. What you buy here
Will not compare to New York City's best.
But it is all you desire at this moment.
It is sufficient.
She leans to present you the warm sack.
Your sterile-gloved fingers touch hers.
Appreciate you more than you know, she says.
In the old Texas way, she appends: Sweetie.
Desire fills your car on the long ride home.
There you strip layers down to parted roll.
Lips of brined brisket unfold to offer
The spicy mustard secreted within.

Eighteen Wheelers and Hope

Eighteen wheelers and hope
Collide on tortured concrete.
Leaving Oklahoma you saw
A dead man on cardboard
In a parking garage.
No being can abide this world.

You navigate and transfer
Amidst cars in tow and
Autobuses aimed toward Mexico.
You plead you will not bleed out here.
Driving is your nirvana:
Dishonest eyes,
Your karma unmerited.

Betrayal Creek Antidote

These fantasies:
Today it is a hotel room,
Maybe Tucson
Maybe some other place.
A shaft of gray light
Intrudes the blinds
And puddles on clothes
Discarded last night.
You feel her breath
On your shoulder,
Someone new —
A woman still unimagined.
Her eyes will be honest.
That you understand.
You'll hail room service
And take time,
No agenda, no deadlines:
The grace of embracing
Unfolding motion.

Hired Hand on Good Friday

In plague and sorrow,
You ride face cloth covered
To dead sands and rock spires
Named for cathedral pipes.
If God's kingdom exists
It is here amidst highways
And shopping centers.
Saints and angels work
At fast food windows
And topless joints — dancers
Available at two-for-one,
Social distancing unrequired.
You opt to seclude in confessional
To release Betrayal Creek sins.
That night you scrutinize
The *Hired Hand* once more.
You become Severn Darden
Fallen from Friday crucifixion.
You slip on your own blood
Leaking from Mexican boots.
Now your stigmata glue these keys.
Typing is all but impossible.
She liked Bruce Langhorne's score —
Concede her that much.
But your movie left her disoriented:
A copperhead striking at shadows.

August 3, 2019

Your cedar elm surrenders its first dead leaves
In this day's white heat. Bushels will follow
By the time December arrives. You stand alone,
Tree litter in your hair, facing disunion and discharge.
In El Paso people you love weep over slaughter.
No recovery: Just loss after loss
At blood-smeared Wal-Mart, lives surrendered
In horror wrought by lethal imageboard.
Your grief cements you in place.
This tree discards your tears.
The tale unfolds: Another nerd white boy —
Eight hours a day plugged in to hate algorithms,
Sabers, swords, and *Game of Thrones* caprices,
Legal purchase, no previous criminal record,
Family never saw it coming . . .

You own no solutions.

False Distant Thunder

Sleep strangled night/Sacred dawn:
You drink more now than ever.
God rests in blue agave.
God is a feral parrot.

You hear false distant thunder.
No mystery here.
Next: sirens and lights,
Then police tape, directed traffic.

You avoid regular routes.
They have taken you nowhere.
You will never drive south
Into counterfeit ardor again.

Tabernacle Shadow

You navigate with eyes shut,
Have for months,
Betrayal Creek disillusion
Still shadow cloaked.
You introduce *The Wild Bunch*
In Salt Lake City,
Then prospect sleep
At a famous motel,
Never detecting motherlode.
Driving the next morning
Along snow highways
Through passages unvisited
In more than thirty years,
You edge along Book Cliffs,
Cretaceous literature desert high.
Next it is onward to Moab's
Ancient cinema before revisiting
LDS tabernacle shadow —
Marriott shelter,
Airport adjacent:
Hot water, firm beds
Forever define Moksha.

Breakdown Tattoos

You stood naked in morning light.
It streamed in Betrayal Creek house
Through plantation shutters.

You were clean.
Track marks like ancient pox scars
Lined her forehead. You failed to see.
You did not yearn for the tangible.

Two overfed cats stared at you
And the hardwood floor felt
Like enamel against your feet.
Everything seemed easy.
You needed this hip pocket gospel.
You convinced yourself
She bore deliverance.

Then memory collapsed the knees.

You recalled a grave robber
Who once prowled these walls —
Sulfur breath, switchblade nails.
Not you, not not you:
Suzuki once more.

You checked your hands for stains:
Breakdown tattoos persevered.

Halfmoon on an Empty Night

Sam Peckinpah destroyed
Every woman he loved
Except his mother,
Who shattered herself
With Christian Science
And mirror worship.

You damaged women in your time.
Your name is alum on their tongues.
But your destructive time finally ran out.
You forged amends with bloodied knees.

Now you seek a woman
Detached from perfection
Both in soul and body
But in all ways authentic:
A halfmoon on an empty night
Who can keep you on the highway,
The only illumination required.

Mirror House

You peel off dusty Levi's and muddy boots
After carnival and revolution winddown.
You own accord with Chet Powers and Pancho Villa.
Nothing lingers from this ride.
You pop the pearl snaps of your Panhandle Slim
And remove sweat soaked socks and briefs —
Naked now, save for tattoos:
Photographic ink of buffalo, peyote buds,
And the last portrait of Quanah Parker.
You walk across an empty midway
To the House of Mirrors.
You switch on one thousand images of yourself.
Some are hardened and scarred.
One is a run-over puppy.
Most are card sharps and bank swindlers
And a man stumbling drunk on his self-fury.
You see Gary Busey. You see Robbie Robertson.
You see Jodi Foster.
Lesions unmedicated swell with pus in every view.
The smartest human you know is a Jersey woman
With 1990s hair and careful eyes.
She once asked, Why build so many fences?
Why write so many ouch poems?
You must own your deconstruction.
You floor drop and hug your knees.
Outside owls scream for the first time.

El Valle

I.

You are a cattle hand
Working the McAllen Ranch
In August heat and dust.
It is 1915 or maybe 2020.
No tags matter.
Time is not pan largo.
It is caldo:
Yesterday, today, tomorrow
All the same.
You wear boots from Raymondville
And a flat-brimmed Stetson.
Your horse is sorrel, high in the hocks,
Splendid for cutting steers.
With Bluetooth earbuds from Amazon
You listen to Dave Alvin & the Blasters
Extolling border radio virtues.
Sometimes you pick up radio dispatches
Concerning the death of Orozco
At High Lonesome, far up the river.
He was an evil metodista.
He was better than the men
Who shot him in the Van Horns.
Gunpowder fouls Valley air too.
It drifts above Betrayal Creek,
Unheeded.

II.

Your life plays out like a Kirk Douglas Western.
Sheriff Stribling says you shot a man in the back.
He says the sun blinded that man.
The sheriff wants to take you to Frio County.
He wants you to hang. You are innocent (this time).
But Siestadera scaffolds mean nothing to you.
You suffered worse at Betrayal Creek.
You and other lost cowhands shot up Bigfoot.
But you owned it, then eased out of town.
You hid nothing.
So be it if Frio City is not placated.
Dying is a shoulder shrug. Buzzard bait is fine destiny.
You were born dead anyway.
Sheriff Stribling flashes Rock Hudson brown eyes.
He breaks Dalton Trumbo's script.
Head south, he says, all the way to Cameron County:
Never cross north of La Mota de Falfurrias again.
You ease your steed into a cantor.
Robert Aldrich is plenty pissed. You cannot care.
You ride out of his widescreen frame.

III.

Aldrich became president of DGA.
He stood up for Sam Peckinpah.
No one else would at that time.
Accord Aldrich that much and more.
He directed *Ulzana's Raid.*
He directed *Emperor of the North Pole.*
He understood corrupted souls.
He could have filmed Betrayal Creek.

IV.

Betrayal Creek is far to the north.
Nightmare turf — you push it away.
You and other drovers drink mezcal.
The cantina is dirty and loud.
It is perfect.
You swap stories about revolution
South of the Río Bravo.
The mezcal waltzes your brain.
You fall from your horse twice
On the way back to the ranch.
Finally you tether your ride.
You stretch out to sleep
With scorpions and snakes
On dirt beneath a quarter moon,
Miles from anywhere,
In the center of everything.
Daybreak voices awaken you.
Down the trail two Rangers
Hold two Tejanos at gunpoint.
Quail coveys erupt with discharge.
The Rangers ride away singing.
You stumble to bodies in mesquite.
The backs of their skulls are missing.
You knew them both:
A teacher, a journalist,
Good men from Brownsville.
At Betrayal Creek, she disdained
Concern for such human beings.
She craved late-night comedy.

V.

You recollect that slice of grace:
Saturday night and Terry Allen
At the Paramount in Austin.
Drinks beforehand with good people:
Guy Clark's sisters, Joe and Sharon Ely,
Dick and Janie DeGuerin, Connie Nelson.
Then a reception afterward: Terry is there.
You chat with Charlie Sexton.
You tell Richard Bowden how much
His fiddling has meant over the years.
You are with your friend Lisa Wade.
You both have suffered losses,
Hers mountainous compared to yours.
The evening unwinds with 1 a.m.
Conversation in her driveway.
You cannot relate what you saw
That night outside Brownsville.
You walk her to the door.
Then you drive to Blue Motel
For six hours of blessed sleep.
The next morning you lead
Your horse from the trailer
And saddle up for the hard ride
Back to the ranch in El Valle.

VI.

A fat man who still speaks with a brogue
Imprisons a 13-year-old Mexicana
As his concubine in the blanched house.
Una vieja mujer must clean and cook for them.
She cares for the girl the best that she can.
The white cow hands who work for him
Snicker and cast glances at shaded windows.
The girl's family in Tamaulipas assembles cash,
Enough to hire eleven vaqueros.
They ride north and cross the river
On a mission of rescue.
Ranch-house siege unfolds as you arrive.
Night wheezes black powder smoke.
It blots stars, condemns the moon.
Your decision is made for you.
You spur with the charros
And begin to fire your hogleg Colt
At the fat man's barricaded windows.
You picture the girl tied, convulsing
And locked in a closet. She must be freed.
But not tonight.
Cartridges run low. Los Rinches close in.
You and los Huastecos gallop into the brush.
You are bullet nicked and weep blood.
Your heart is failure crushed.
The woman at Betrayal Creek vapes weed
On the love seat with her scientist.
They giggle and stream *Between Two Ferns*.

Years Before

I.

Years before you witnessed her staged face,
You drove every night from Belton
To Fort Hood, gold globes suspended
In air as troops rehearsed
The great Soviet war
That never came.

Years before you ever heard of Betrayal Creek,
You played a cassette of the newest Los Lobos
In your old pickup
As you entered post and drove
To a set of temporary buildings
Where you taught things like
Effective Army Communications.
Skunks frequently invaded
With the hot midnight winds.

Los Lobos sang of riverbeds
And red-tail hawks circling
When it was time to go.

II.

Years before she and you first had sex
In a car in the shadow of Austin's
Mount Bonnell (people everywhere),
You were on post when the Gulf War
Erupted and nothing was the same.
Tanks and armored personnel carriers
Hastily painted to mimic desert sand
Dried nipple pink on railcars
Rolling toward the Port of Houston.

The newest Los Lobos album
Turned a month old.
T-Bone Burnett made you proud
To be Texan.

III.

Years before you ingested her savor,
You heard rumors that Iraqi agents
Planned to blow up the post Burger King
As if the hamburgers there weren't
Terrifying enough on their own.
You learned just how depressed you were
When you discovered your wife slept
With a lieutenant colonel
And you didn't give a damn.

IV.

Years before she led you through twisted tunnels,
You fled post early and went to a concert
By Little Joe y La Familia and Ruben Ramos.
You might have been the only white person there.
It was good to be in a sane place.

Bell County, Texas, set a record for divorces
With virtually all of Fort Hood's troops
In Kuwait and Iraq.
You trained MPs, who told you
Crips and Bloods infiltrated
The Army and stole
Rocket launchers
And other weapons.

A moron attempted
To mail a camel head
To Copperas Cove.

You met a massage therapist
Who said she liked gay porn.

Sometimes you listened
To "Down on the Riverbed"
A dozen times in a row.
Louie Pérez, David Hidalgo, yes!
A monster cloud...

V.

Years before she intubated you with herself
And allowed you to relinquish flesh and skull,
You wagered all in a Bell County-born
Ghoul game and survived by tooth skin.
The river by your house ran cottonmouth thick.
But you saw Little Joe on Sundays at H-E-B
And that gave you a lift. But you learned nothing.

You married again, this time to a woman
Who hated Los Lobos.
Why? You have no words.
She wanted a church on a hill.
You wanted tequila and pale blue nights.
Divorcing that wife took forever...

The years expire.
You are resolute.

Terry Allen's Mother

Terry Allen's mother was expelled
From SMU for making music
With a black jazz band in the 1920s.
You hear that piano
And feel that tenor sax weep
In forbidden Deep Ellum venue.
Terry Allen later sold set ups
At B.B. King dances and
Ernest Tubb jamborees.
Later still he consumed Kerouac
And Hemingway.
The result: *Lubbock (On Everything)*.
You heard it as a crushed soul
Oklahoma kid, now dead and gone,
Reborn in Texas caliche.

Resurrection means
Wearing cowboy boots
While reading Suzuki, Lao-Tze
And Oscar Zeta Acosta.
You ponder planting Mexican plums
On property you cannot possess.

The Last Movie

I.

You watch
The Last Movie
For the first time
In twenty years.
You freeze a frame
Of Peruvian sunset
And think about
The plains where
You grew up — 1970
And you were fourteen
And forgot to return
A record club card.
An album called
Kristofferson arrives
At your parents' P.O. box.
You are stuck with it.
Thank everything holy
For your neglect:
You listened
Obsessively.

II.

Here on the screen now
Is Kristofferson, so young,
Growling with Hopper
In *The Last Movie*, which is
An ode, I heard a woman say,
To threatened white men
Of his generation
Swinging their penises
In public while pretending
To be Jesus Christ.
You cannot disagree.
Still you value the film
Because it makes no sense.
You celebrate Kristofferson's album
Because it makes total sense.
Always has.
You reflect on Sunday mornings
At Betrayal Creek, no coming down.
Just slow, sunny moments
Of bacon, eggs, tea, and conversation
Between two stricken people
Clouded by self-deception
But leaning on each other.

Rodney Crowell

I.

You recollect that month of grace and trust:
Four concerts, four weeks — X, Wilco,
Willis Alan Ramsey, and Rodney Crowell.
Rodney was joint communion for you both,
World never born, never ceasing, amen.
That night in a South Austin prayer house
He heralded and bemoaned
Expensive tequila and chinaberry sidewalks,
Boozing dads and Bible-thumping mothers,
Passion and refinery toxic drifts,
DDT clouds and beer joint busted knuckles.

Rodney composed your score and gospel.
Betrayal Creek's woman knew and abetted.
That music was concrete for you both
During your own dumpster fire days —
When you imploded all that you touched.

II.

¿Cómo acumulé este milagro?

Soy un hombre afortunado
Soy un hombre de viento y lluvia
Soy un hombre enamorado
Soy un hombre que ha sido bendecido

The Houston Kid
No habla español pero
El entiende cada palabra

You embraced miracles for sure
During those ecstasy weeks.
You never allowed your eyes to see
The open wounds on her face.
You returned to the cancer ward
And mistook metastasis for love.

III.

You read about the next virus assault.
It will be worse than this pandemic.
It will collapse hospitals and clinics.
No one can be safe.
You remember Rodney's song for the life.
You both wept as he sought
To gain control again.
Just so: Your real father is enigma.
Your mother has lied about him for decades.
He is a rodeo cowboy but not the one you know.
The woman next to you now wove falsity too.
You have produced your own.
You have never owned sanctuary.
That is your doing, not hers, not anyone else's.

You wanted Rodney to sing of highways
Lonesome and long. Not tonight.
You conjured your own collapse and arson
On the drive back to Betrayal Creek.

Native Primrose

This morning you savored Wolf Moon,
New poetry by Red Shuttleworth,
That kind, good man. Then came litanies
To Emilio Fernández's *Víctimas del pecado*,
Mexican noir, superb in craft, art —
Ninón Sevilla's voice chanting still,
Five years after her death.
You understand everyone falls to sin,
Even skeptics such as yourself.
Now you shovel a fissure in gumbo,
This sacred Texas black earth.
You fill it with offering: native primrose.
Soon it will crowd your window
With satisfactory blossoms.
You have failed at love time and again.
An image of Betrayal Creek's woman
Trespasses in the mind and halts your labor.
You lean your collapsing handle
To consider her ancient distension.
You wish her amity and rescue,
Then renew dirt work in the sun.

Permeation

Up there night fell as a hangman's collar.
The cold permeated stone and glass
As if they were no more than oxygen.
You witnessed quarter moon tragedy.

She danced far away under palms.
You remained behind with doubt and gales.
How could anyone love me?
You stood above a black corner arroyo.

You once read all of John Berryman.
Delusions Etc. became your tramp stamp.
No one spoke to you of wisdom and rivers.
Her house was locked and you owned no key.

Drunk and stoned, jaundiced on the rich coast,
Betrayal Creek's woman extended nothing.

Days of the Dead

White people forsook
The ability to see the dead
Walking among us
Two thousand years ago.

Why did you breed
It out of yourself?

In yesterday's chilly sunshine,
Niños constructed ofrenditas
To invite los angelitos to return.
Today is Día de los Inocentes.
Children no longer alive are here
To laugh and play games
While munching sugar skulls.

Mañana: Día de los Difuntos.
Graves will be clean
Along Brushy Creek,
Decorated with twenty flowers,
Pan de muerto next to headstones.
You will deposit a bottle of Old Forester
Above Sam Bass's fossilizing bones
And empty El Presidente brandy
On the earth for los otros.

Next year you will travel
To Juchitán de Zaragoza.

Winterkill

Obscenity of Halloween freeze
At your place in south Central Texas:

Lantana will be as black and broken
As the winterkill love in this house.
You cannot find warmth.

Roofers' nail guns like fireworks
On Independence Day
At the house behind you —
A piercing reminder of better days.

July must be a century past.

You hammered yourself.
This failure is yours
And must be owned.
You never opened shutters.
You were content in the dark:
A brown recluse in the closet.

Resurrection

While driving north from Betrayal Creek
You listen to Kinky Friedman's "Resurrection,"
A song about Tom Baker, among others —
Tom Baker, star of Warhol's *I, A Man*,
Dead forty years, almost.
Almost all the Superstars are gone now.
Even old Harold Stevenson died
In Oklahoma last year, aged eighty-nine.
You thought he'd somehow live forever —
Idabel boy who'd painted
An 8x39 foot mural of a naked man,
Sal Mineo as the model,
First exhibited at a Paris gallery —
Yes, Harold Stevenson walked on,
Departing from where he started,
Idabel in the Choctaw Nation.
You recall he mentored your first wife's cousin,
Robert, whom you knew when he rodeoed
And painted like crazy, broke most of the time.
Now as Poteet Victory he's a Santa Fe success.
You dispute if there is any real resurrection,
But you love Kinky's songs.
And you're glad Robert made it.
You never want to see eighty-nine
And plead to be topsoil long before then.

Nolte

Thirty-three miles from Betrayal Creek
You position for cold drizzle and wind yowl.

You read an obscure book about Nick Nolte
And wonder if he and Peckinpah

Could have collaborated on pictures,
Two men with logic and temper issues,

Both of them wing-stripped fighter pilots
Battling vanity wars and producers,

Both night-stunned alcoholics:
Betrayal Creek's woman is a drunk.

You question if you are one as well.
Each night's sleep is tequila lubricated.

Everyone botches the dog soldier path.

1:30 A.M. Words after the Death of a Beloved Cat

Little to say except misery is
A chair fashioned from doorknobs
And loss is a fall Taos gorge deep.
Even though you know it to be untrue
You sense despair has no final credits.
That movie seems to play forever,
No way to edit it.

You swallow a second tequila.

Why more grief for pets than humans?
Are you defective in some way?
Only in that you deny yourself wailing.
It is time appropriate for howling
To the roofbeam, stomping floor holes,
And smashing furniture.

You curtail too much, always have.

At Valentina's

You are returned from San Antonio,
Kicked back in Manchaca now
Maybe three miles from Betrayal Creek.
A man marches along the road in black,
Barefoot, eight-foot length of PVC pipe
His bearing cross:
El Hermano de la Fraternidad Piadosa
De Nuestro Padre Jesús Nazareno in bubba-land
Strolling onward toward Good Friday flagellation
Still months away. You care not for religion,
But you feel sanctified here on this earth,
Woodsmoke wafting like cathedral incense
At Valentina's Tex Mex BBQ, hecho con amor.

Hemorrhaged Sunsets

In Tucson you found the right saloon
Stuck at the back of a famous hotel,
Only a bar and several small tables.
No abominable karaoke here,
Just a dusty Wurlitzer from '74.
And, yes, there were Gary Stewart 45s
Along with Dolly Parton and Conway Twitty:
Music turned low, conversations relaxed.

You thought you could live in that city with her:
Javelinas, rattlesnakes, Pancho Villa statue,
Postcard dawns and hemorrhaged sunsets,
El Charro Café with Mo Udall hearth,
Carne seca platter and tequila,
Saguaros on every mountainside.

But you were moment-lost in the desert.
You neglected to heed her gashes,
Some inflicted by men, some self-lacerated,
All as bloody as the Arizona dusks.

You are glad you are not drunk tonight.
A coiled western diamondback awaits
In the dark outside your house in Texas.
This is your world. This is what you know.

Cleaning Day

Gaby arrives with helpers
At a house that is emptier
Than it has been in fifteen years.

She speaks Spanish, as always:
¿Dónde está tu gato?
Está muerta.
¡O no!
Si, estoy muy triste...

Gaby comes from Laredo.
She returns home often,
Sometimes for tattoo work.
Her arms are exquisite
Canvases in Mexican style:
Flowers, shrubs, and trees
With hidden eyes.

Once her daughter said:
My mother thinks you are
A high school Spanish teacher.
Un cumplido de hecho.
Los maestros are esteemed
In Gaby's place and culture.

You watch her dust blinds.
You could have been more.

Sober

You understand the importance
Of sobering up after total
Intoxication.
It is true for tequila binges,
The same for infatuation.
Betrayal Creek's woman
Led you aswirl
For seven months.
Hard light shines down.
You absorb everything now:
Roads with potted asphalt,
Nearby houses burglarized,
Traffic resisting cure,
Sudden ice in her kisses.

Coming from a Place of Honesty

Your mother compulsively perjured herself.
Your grandmother gave birth to a child
When she was fifteen.
She told no one about it.
Your last wife was shallow
And a Bible thumper who was obsessed
With royal weddings on television.
Your first wife lied about oil leases.
The smartest person you know
Scolds you for your lack of trust,
Yet she concedes she understands.
She stresses forgiveness —
A calculus that befuddles you.
Tomorrow is Daddy-O's memorial.
You will weep in front of the multitude.
You loathe electrical engineers
Because one torpedoed your life.
You are glad Warren Oates died
Before he witnessed this digital morass.
You never want your wrist to vibrate
With a fucking Apple watch.
You should have been born
A Durango charro a century ago.
I was a Durango charro. . .
You cannot assuage the spikes
You stumble on in this world.
Thank god for Joe "King" Carrasco
Who will sing Daddy-O's goodbye
At a castle afloat above Austin.

Daddy-o Is Dead

Three days later
And you sit alone
Listening to
Curtis Mayfield,
Superfly,
Wishing it could be
1972 all over again.
Freddie's dead.

Daddy-O is dead too,
The news plastered
Across a globe
Crowded yet empty
Of burning souls.
You are sick of hollow.

No one coached you
For this frozen slide
And dispelled hope.
Courage is discarded
Plastic drive-in cups
In morning frost.

Hair Curled Tight

No one ever offered
To take care of you —
And now even sound
Regresses
To empty couch
And shadowless walls.

Nothing is more wretched
Than Saturday night
With a woman
No longer in love.

Soka Gakkai Failure

Soka Gakkai on a
Leafless tree night,
But practice fails.
You spend seven hours
Sleepless in pain
Reading Patti Smith's
Year of the Monkey,
Charles Olson's
Call Me Ishmael,
And Glenn Shirley's
Cowboy/outlaw book
West of Hell's Fringe.
You cannot smell recovery
In this Airstream.

You are a 1987 Chevy Impala —
Tires bald, shocks shot.
Too many highways,
Too many hailstorms
In West Texas —
You crave rusting away.

Clouds over Denver (Again)

You jet in clouds over Denver,
Southwest Airlines tequila
On the chair-back tray,
Earbud Sones Jarochos
Making you feel like fleeing
This Boeing 737-800
For the cumulus baile outside.
Tucson rests five hours behind,
Ciudad que ambos amamos,
City of breath and blood.
A flight attendant asks
If you are okay.
How to explain
Bee-loud desert gardens —
Apologies to Yeats —
Or the naked unwrapping of
Sonoran sunrises?
A saguaro-encrusted mountain pass
Became your vow and deliverance.

Another Death

Another day, another death,
Welcome to your new world.
The smartest person you know is
Silent and why not?
She can say nothing.
November was your best month.
December devolved into nightmare.
Your new merit badge:
Betrayal survivor.
It's no different from your first.

You ponder buying
A Quetzalcoatl Serpent t-shirt,
No maybe Tlaloc is better,
The water god/the storm god.
Clothed in his image
You'll wade the muddy Gulf
At Port O'Connor
And trudge your way
To honest baptism.

Frozen Fog

First trip in six months
Without her —
You remember a wasted age
When you preferred things
This way/no longer.
You sweat Oklahoma
Winter nights
Craving her body
Next to yours.
Predawn darkness
And you step outside
Into frozen fog
Far from Betrayal Creek.

Clean Habitation

You drive streets in sunshine gild.
You know and do not know this place.
It is both strange and familiar,
An old man in hospice now,
Strangling in death shadow
Yet somehow still alive.
That is your little town,
Guthrie, Oklahoma.
You climb hospital hill.
For decades the brick and mortar
That witnessed your first breath
Sat abandoned and disregarded except
For ghost hunters
Graffiti taggers
And skateboarders.
Now it is refurbished
As senior citizen cubicles,
A clean habitation
For happy dying.
You pray to a god you deny
Please do not check me in,
Not here, not this way.
A skein of mutant geese
Glides above you at noon.

Spiny Lizard

Today is a good day to die.
It is also a good day to live.
Too often you neglect the latter
And obsess about the former.
You witness two Texas spiny lizards
Alert among coral yuccas.
Reptiles have possessed this earth
Much longer than you. They survive.
These females lay twenty-five eggs
In nests burrowed into the ground.
They do this several times a year.
Profiting means nothing to them.
It is endurance that matters.

You take your place on agave leaves
And rustle your scales for the sun.

Sockets and Handles

When you were a child you spake as a child
But listened up as oilfield drillers told you
A man needs a woman like an octopus needs
A set of Snap-on sockets and wrench handles.
Snap-on tools, they'd add, are the world's best.
You never understood the why of that coda.
After the Old Man died, your mother gave you
A box of his rescued tools: They were Snap-on,
Of course: Yours came from Sears.

You start today with a four-mile Brushy Creek run.
Next: five hours nonstop under the Texas sun.
Manning mower and chainsaw. Hoeing, shoveling.
Hustling fifty-pound bags of wet mulch.
Shirtless in shorts and ancient sneakers,
Silver bandana binding your skull,
You renew your claim to this swatch of earth.
But you sweat and work alone, as always.
You now realize this is travesty.
Sockets have no value minus handles.

Unplugging

In the midst of pestilence Kourtney Kardashian
Poses in a bikini next to a luxury pool.
This is news. This is America.
A New York emergency room doctor kills herself
Because of people dying before they exit ambulances.
So many stricken, so many corpses —
We have gone medieval on ourselves.
No one cares much. Let them feast on Twitter.
You think of Sam Peckinpah
In *Invasion of the Body Snatchers*.
You understand now how horror works:
Humans become pods by way of social media.
Pod people now outnumber us ten thousand to one.
Or maybe it is a hundred thousand. . .
You recall the way Betrayal Creek's woman was
Wired and Bluetoothed — dating app addicted,
Hopped up on secret Facebook groups,
Rivetted by Instagram posts,
Apple Watch buzzing away through the night.
You have pelted her with scorn, anger, dismissal.
You regret that. She needed a meeting address
And recitation for serenity. Maybe she'll find it.
You sit alone under a halfmoon, no device at hand.
A breeze promises midnight renewal and rain.
You hum along with a great horned owl duet
From off toward Brushy Creek.

Heat

You crave August heat.
You hate winter shortened days.
No slate skies, no rusted leaves,
You require sweat burning eyes,
Cracked soil, furnace blast south wind,
And insect cries from summer trees.
You want sidewalk fire searing soles
When you run at two in the afternoon
To drive you coherent.

Carcass Drift

Carcass drift in ebbing times —
Death is much with you this night.
You know cut earth smells from a new grave.
You know evaporation of the innocent.

You can scarcely breathe these days.
Pathetic porn of politics and social media
Overwhelms, depletes, diminishes,
And augers nothing more than dust.

We have little time remaining on this stone.
Our capacity is short-circuited.
Our future? Ashes or a hole in the ground.
Saviors are only bleach-beard hustlers.

You remember her secret Facebook politics.
She never understood her cacophony.

Country Feedback

I.

When bleeding supersedes. . .

You recollect corroded months
When you galloped insane
In northwest Austin.

You listened to R.E.M.'s
"Country Feedback"
As if it could restore decay —
Almost thirty years ago
Out of Time on cassette.
Crazy
Crazy
Crazy

Your brain was a steel guitar.
Michael Stipe was the rabbi:
Only he knows this story.

II.

Crazy at the cocaine company,
Stolen mail lists, ethics flushed
USPS investigations,
Forged receipts, false claims —
We underlings had no peace
Except headphone music.

You recall flying to Denver on United
With a dark-haired young woman,
Baptist vows lost at Larimer Square.

You recall another woman
Who overhauled engines
While wearing your class ring.

Her face is fogged glass now.
She'd once been a cop,
Carried a .357 Magnum
Everywhere she went.
You never doubted she'd use it.

III.

Scene Missing. . .

Film on:
You thought you were rising.

But you began a grackle dive
Into lightless caverns.
All used up, you lost your eyes,
And ended up back in Bell County.

You surrendered to Jesus People
Who ran convenience stores:
The Gospel and Trinity
Of cigarettes, oil and gas,
And jack off magazines.

A VP took you aside and said
Sign up with Promise Keepers
And you'll go far here. . .

You shuddered and wept at night
As good Christians dressed well
And abandoned their children.

Devout Baptists bedded each other
And played church league basketball.

IV.

You tossed your brain in Jesus Town.

Sometimes you secured yourself
In storeroom darkness
To sweat and shiver.
Even there you turned to
"Country Feedback"
On your worn-out Walkman.
At an apartment you flayed
Your youth too soon,
Lost in I-35 ruckus.

Excuses why you did it:
I could not talk about it.
I could not even think it.

Across the parking lot,
A Scott & White nurse
Disrobed every night
And fondled herself
In front of exposed glass
As a dozen men gawked.
You stood among them.

V.

You went to see a shrink
Who wore a white lab coat
And proffered self-help.

He said your IQ was
The highest he'd recorded.
Why are you in Temple, Texas?
He fingered his bleached lapel
And waited for an answer.
You managed only a shrug.
He said abandon this town.
He also recommended Tai Chi.

VI.

You never joined Promise Keepers.
You fled just before you were fired.
You returned to Austin in time
To fashion a twenty-year nightmare
Of hotel room and parking lot dates
While working high tech —
All leading to Betrayal Creek.

Crazy

Dennis Hopper at Mueller

Dennis Hopper waltzed Mueller airport halls —
Tequila breath, cocaine mustache, reeking,
Busted lips, black-eyed, lost but still seeking
Divination from Richard Nixon walls.
He leaned on Eddie, who lamented stalls
And pushed Dennis onward, sometimes taking
Salvation from spent deeds that came sneaking
From old gas stations, windshields, and night crawls.

You wish you could have been around back then:
Free, insane, eternally holistic
Tripping frantic yellow armadillos.
But you are here now alive and open.
You are flesh, you are real, you are mystic.
You plead eternal as cobalt sky billows.

Albuquerque

You listen to 1975 Neil Young
And drift back to a March day
At an airport hotel
In Albuquerque.
Slow Sheraton heat
Kept the room
Almost tolerable.
Downstairs
Southwest pilots
And flight attendants
Drank in a weeping bar.

Max Evans was too sick
To meet for lunch.
You stood susceptible at a
Window pondering
Southwest's next takeoff,
But you held steady.
Snowflake-blurred lights
Burned beyond the blinds.
Inside that room
You professed no religion
Except screwbean mesquite
And western soapberry leaves
Scattered across carpet.

Courage of Listening

What fails the eye can be deadly.
A forestalled vent is often
Undetectable even in light.
The gale builds and builds
Until a blast is inevitable.
Wind must gust at times
Unimpeded.
It took you decades
To learn that trying to direct it
Will prove to be biased folly.
Always, always.
It requires courage to curtail impulse.
You hand sit and move to words.
You are not a coyote of the field.
You are human for once.

Integrity

Driving down the toll road
Keeping lines thin, hard,
Listening to Lukas Nelson
And the Promise of the Real
As horizons bleed birth
Of December dawn,
You embrace paying to move.
You dodged too many fares
On too many turnpikes
For too many decades.
Now all accounts balance.
You are shameless in showing
Your statements to anyone.
Morning is clear and cold,
And you are rolling,
No longer in arrears.

Panadería Juárez

Dead cricket sidewalk morning
And you arrive at the panadería
Y restaurante as early Mass
Bells peal down the street.
She stands behind the counter,
First time in months, and smiles.
Her face is still thin and well-scrubbed.
The only change: a new nose ring.
"I took a job at H-E-B," she says,
"But they didn't give me enough hours.
So I'm back." Her life is a poem. You say:
¡Me alegro de que hayas regresado!
"Yeah, me too!" she says. "It's good
To see you again." You carry tortillas
And coffee outside. Wind picks up.
Insect husks skitter across concrete.
Resurrection bells fall quiet.

Sunlight

You read poetry by ire'ne lara silva
And Emmy Pérez
While listening to Lisa Morales.
You recall her and Paul Ramírez
Performing in South Austin
During autumn weeks of work
And transcendence,
A perfect soundtrack for those times
As well as today.
The woman who sat next to you then
No longer feels or desires anything
For or from you,
Her prerogative, and that is suitable,
Just as it is yours to liberate
The caged fighting cocks in your brain.
You have learned the unperformed
Song called "El Perdón."
Sunlight outside your window beckons.
You knot bandana, find shades, and waltz
Outdoors to replant Mexican petunias.

Laid Off, March 2020

No job for the first time in thirty years —
You face it well, publicly, but you slide
Behind locked doors and surrender to fears
Of no recovery. All that you hide

Glares from the mirror in this silent room.
Eyes soldered shut and yet you can still see
Failure like poison cloth from a dead loom.
It strangles you, pulls at your sanity.

You deposit your scars on this counter
Along with toothpaste and shaving lather,
Then flush away this rancid encounter.
You own no endings. Instead you gather

Light from an El Paso woman's strong face.
Her abrazos lift you from this harsh space.

Parched Heart Remedy

With sanction sex never fails
Even at its least.

At a minimum it is as good as October
Daybreaks in Taos.

At best it exceeds Beethoven in layering
And in texturing.

At times it is something greater still:

Neruda's el agua de un río que desemboca
En mi corazón calcinado.

You can claim it.

Darkness, Darkness

I.

A song by a band that interests you
Only marginally.

A song produced by Charlie Daniels
In pre-reactionary days.

A song from an album with better reputation
Than it merits.

A song with fiddle by David Lindley
Yearning gloom.

A song knowing pain, emptiness
And cold shadows. . .
Yes, you have been there.
That dark arroyo.

The song is the only soundtrack
Suitable for this episode.

II.

Sanity: You thought you owned it.
Driving past homeless tents
Below overpasses in Silverlake,
Thinking: You are not the one
Stretched out in filthy sleeping bags,
You are not the one eating Mexican meth
Teeth falling out.
You held that notion never knowing
It's just an eyelash away, just an eyelash,
For any of us

Your Phaedrus was the sane one,
Never mind shock therapy
And lobotomy talk.
You never understood
Your Narrator was the ghoul
Who haunted Betrayal Creek
Wreaking sorrow.
You thought he was normal
But he was psychotic:
Liar/deceiver/manipulator
Surfing forever into boundless night
Proclaiming he was the light.

It is not easy to write these things.

III.

You speak here of collapse,
Not burn and pillage,
But simple folding and hurt.
It hit one Betrayal Creek night,
Thanksgiving of all times.

Welcome home, she said,
Vodka on her breath
And why not?
You had betrayed her
Yourself more than once.

You understood vodka
As resilience and calm.

You dived headlong into yourself
And lost all memory
Of what occurred that night.

You did your own tossing aside
In fog and torment.

IV.

She moved on, made a turn
And forged life without you.

Emptiness swallowed you.
Self-loathing was your sole mantra.
It kept your mind away from things
That could not be and maybe never were.

Fourth-floor conference room at National
Obsessed you: Maybe unspool
The beating coil behind that door?
Model 40 10mm Glock always at the ready.
Some work friends used that room
For Muslim prayer.
Their kindness and humor eliminated
That space from any conclusions.

V.

You studied Spanish daily, even days
When you had colonoscopies,
Even Christmas, especially Christmas.

You took to wearing a thirty-year-old
Levi's trucker jacket and listened
To Mexican music endlessly.

One day you played "El Chuchumbé"
By White Monkey Group
Twenty-seven times in a row —
A song once church-banned.

El Chuchumbé:
Region of a man's body
Five inches below the navel:
It brought you joy and woe.

You tried translating a biography
Of Emilio Fernández
By Paco Ignacio Taibo I.
You failed. And failed again.

VI.

The smartest person you know watched
Session after session, eyes of sadness,
At moments eyes of desperation.
At other times she prodded and soothed.
Look at me, she'd say
Look at me, look at me.
You did not want to look at anyone
Except the woman at Betrayal Creek.
But you could not say that.
You had locked her away.
One day the smartest person you know said:
Everything happens the way it does
Because it cannot happen any other way.
Lao-Tze whispered agreement over your shoulder.
The smartest person you know
Had traveled down your broken glass highway.
You were both addicts in different attire.
One day she spoke Spanish to you:
Not much but some. It was a life preserver.

VII.

Sometimes you went to therapy three times a week.
You heard about forgiveness of others.
You learned you are rage possessed.
You failed self-compassion.
You could not apologize to yourself.
You were tattooed by depression diagnosis.
You did not give a fuck about your job
But remained employed for months afterward.
You were happy only at the boxing gym:
Your cathedral, your beer joint.
Friends died all around.
You began running again.
You liked the car wash.
You liked the panaderia.
Therapy nearly killed you.
The smartest person you know
Kept you moving with eyes and words.
But you never once mentioned
Berryman's *Dream Songs*
Although you lived them.

VIII.

You compiled a manuscript mess,
Unfixable yet demanding a fix.
The smartest person you know said
You had to push.
You humiliated yourself to friends
You respected. Their edits
Pared muscle from your bones.
So many mistakes, so much shame
But you pushed, you pushed.
One Sunday you started at six a.m.
At ten you opened a fifth of Herradura plato.
Tequila propellant kept you going to one a.m.
The next day you emailed The Wild Bunch to New York.
Now scrubbed, it was the longest and best book
You'd ever written.
How do you feel? the smartest person you know asked.
Peckinpah, Lao-Tze, and San Judas Tadeo
Stood behind her laughing.

IX.

Mystical events occurred.
In Taos, Max Evans told
A man that Peckinpah
Considers you a good friend.
But Kip never met Peckinpah,
The man in Taos said.
I know that, Max said.
Peckinpah says he respects Kip. . .
Thirty-three years after Sam died.

A Lakota named Owns the Saber
Fashioned a Peckinpah lithograph
In a San Francisco basement.
It was rolled in a tube
For more than three decades,
Then mailed to you parcel post.
Wrong address, wrong zip code.
Yet it arrived on your porch just a day
After post office delivery
In Northern California.

Yes, mystical things. . .

X.

Then it happened:

Day by day
The details
Of that gloom
On Thanksgiving
At Betrayal Creek
Began to return.

You came to recall:
Rolling on carpet upstairs,
Shivering through a night
While clutching a pillow,
Declining her offerings,
Staring at morning TV news endlessly,
Shouting into a phone:
I'm broken/I'm broken
The smartest person you know, saying:
I'm broken/She's broken/Everyone is broken.

Two long late-night drives,
Driveway encounters:
Then months of nothing
But misguided anger
And memory loss.

XI.

Own that these things occurred.
But also own that you did your labor.
You made amends. You healed.
But you failed to see that she was
As broken as you ever were.
Maybe more so.
She proved unskilled at her own labor.
Own that too as you step out
Beneath a waxing gibbous phase.
You smell mulch and late mountain laurel
And remember that snakes crawl at night.

Not Henry

Berryman, Henry's brain corner:
White-breasted penguins.
You are urged to sing but refuse.
Never perform impromptu these days.

You sat at the Paramount
Watching and listening to X,
Exene and John Doe together,
Ex-spouses in sync,

As it should be,
As it almost never is.
You celebrate these moments
Free from Henry-like obsession.

You are not Henry, thank God,
Not any longer. The sky is clear.

Red Cadillac

(in memory of Don Spencer)

I.

You drove a red Cadillac.
You didn't own it.
Everyone possessed it.
But it was your turn
Behind that wheel.
You drove a red Cadillac
To Rehoboth Baptist Church
For final rites.
You carried one of the only
White faces mourning.
You crouched into a balcony
With black men
And Mexican couples
All weeping before
A word was spoken.
You drove that Cadillac
To this place
To say goodbye
To a friend
Imploded by cancer.
But you fell into yourself
Among farewell sobs.

II.

You conjured
Betrayal Creek's woman
In the crowded balcony.
You shed tears
For every knife
Ever thrown
Toward anyone.
You drove a red Cadillac
Away from Rehoboth
After the service.
You passed a golf course
And a darkened airport.

III.

For a moment
She sat next to you,
Her hand on yours.
But then was gone.
Though perfume lingered.
Sometimes you think
You were born
To drive a red Cadillac
Through the night.
But you were born to nothing.
You built your own highways.
Your crashes forged wreckage
For many people. Hers did the same.
No guiltless accidents occurred.
You drove a red Cadillac,
Eyes fixed on the center divider,
Speed under control.

What Writers and Editors are Saying about
Betrayal Creek

Stratton's anguished and insistent poems of loss and heartache are raw as the desert wind on a very dark night.

    —Wes Ferguson, Senior Editor, *Texas Monthly*

Betrayal Creek draws anyone who has ever loved and lost into the timeless waters of an "honest baptism" and the resulting courage of a "saddle-scarred soul" to reclaim healing and wholeness. Infused with "The grace of embracing/ Unfolding motion," it is a joy to read and filled with a surprising simplicity of eloquence.

    Stratton's poetry is tangible, immediate, as shimmering and crystal clear as a jigger of something too tough to down in one gulp, but which we feel hungry to swig down anyway. Painted in penetrating images of these Texas-Mexico Borderlands, this exquisitely bare masterpiece takes the reader on a tour of duty through a nasty betrayal and all the echoes of life which preceded it, a brick-by-adobe-brick reconstruction of the very human search for love, for self, and for survival.

    —Carmen Tafolla, State Poet Laureate of Texas 2015

"What happens to a man after a long journey, as a survivor worn and bruised by love, by disasters—some of his own making and others not—and by a desolate landscape that eerily calls him home? W. K. Statton's *Betrayal Creek* mines this battered self for solace, beauty, redemption, anger, even deliverance. The words cut deeply for those who will still pay attention to something as timeless as a saguaro in the desert."

    —Sergio Troncoso, author of *A Peculiar Kind of Immigrant's Son*

Kip Stratton's *Betrayal Creek* is contemporary confessional poetry at its finest. It lays bare the inward landscape of an "ordinary man /

with spurs and a saddle-scarred soul" through a lover's betrayal, into the depths of depression, and finally out into the glorious Texan sunlight beckoning on the other side of a window. What's most striking about these poems is their ability to connect the personal to the universal—the suffering of one man to the suffering of a country in peril. Betrayal Creek grieves the loss of a love, the loss of life amid a global pandemic, and our collective lost humanity at the hands of racism and gun violence. The collection ends with the forlorn yet resilient speaker speeding off into the open road in a red Cadillac, offering a kind of symbolic hope that our world, too, can survive such darkness and emerge wiser, stronger, and scarred.

    —Katherine Hoerth, Poetry Editor, *Amarillo Bay* and author of *Goddess Wears Cowboy Boots*

Kip Stratton's *Betrayal Creek* is a rich, rewarding collection of poems filled with polarities, from the pain of loss and betrayal to the resilience of expectation and yearning. Kip's poems are deeply engaging, filled with quick, subtle shifts from the here and now to the immutable and metaphysical. Deftly crafted and evocative, his poems reveal great emotional depth and erudite discernment.

    —Dan Williams, director, TCU Pres and author of *Past Purgatory, a Distant Paradise*

Betrayal Creek is a rangy collection of hardscrabble poems on the heart, the pieces revealing a wandering spirit in search for "the only love that can be trusted." The poems stand alone individually or may be read as an odyssey, departing from Betrayal Creek, in itself an invented name for Kip's very real loss, but a journey that returns in rawboned images to a home that is always the American West.

    —Jeffrey DeLotto, author of *Voices Writ in Sand: Dramatic Monologues and Other Poems* and *A Caddo's Way*

In these poems Kip Stratton's persona sifts through the emotional debris of a failed relationship, moving slowly from anger and bitterness at the outset toward compassion ("You never allowed your eyes to see/ The open wounds on her face") and ultimate transcendence as he leaves his "broken glass highway" to start anew. Along the way he also examines topics as diverse as the El Paso shootings, ravages of the pandemic, and perils of social media. All who have weathered a heartbreak, and those who have not, will find value in these tightly crafted reflections. I strongly recommend *Betrayal Creek*.

—Carol Reposa, Texas Poet Laureate for 2018 and author of *Underground Musicians*

The opening epigraph from Adrienne Rich's "Diving into the Wreck" warns the reader that what is to come will be a brutal form of confessional therapy. And Stratton's *Betrayal Creek* is indeed that. Using songs and films as his touchstones, he tries to make sense of the duplicity that was always there yet never was recognized except in afterthoughts. As coping skills he employs "Sobriety and lust: / Two ends of the same rope." But nothing, he writes, is more wretched "Than Saturday night / With a woman / No longer in love."

These poems are a record of Stratton's attempts to protect his greatest vulnerabilities. The more he turns inward like a sock, the farther away seems healing. Broken by love's betrayal, he wonders if all romantic relationships—past and future—are fueled by "counterfeit ardor." How is one to know? He turns to tequila, hard labor, therapy, and the ghost of Sam Peckinpaugh (about whom he has previously evocatively written) to ease his discomposure. He lives on life's emotional edge, always on the border. As with every restraint, he yearns to cross it. He thinks bilingually, listens to its conjunto soundtrack. But which way is the frontier? Like all broken-hearted lovers, Stratton finds it impossible to know which way to face and what to turn his back on. What he discovers is there can be no triumph over betrayal. Surviving it will have to be enough.

—Jerry Bradley, Poetry Editor of *Concho River Review* and author of *Collapsing into Possibility*

W.K. (Kip) Stratton is a man of parts. Most recently, he won major awards for his bestselling book, *The Wild Bunch: Sam Peckinpah, a Revolution in Hollywood, and the Making of a Legendary Film*. Stratton has written varied other works, including three books of poetry. But this new volume, *Betrayal Creek*, steps away from the accolades and comes from a place of sorrow and disappointment--a cri de coeur about a relationship gone bad. These poems speak from a place of sadness and regret that many will recognize. Stratton's new collection reaches into the heart with a vibrant humanity that lifts readers' understanding of the height and depth of human experience.

—Mark Busby, Distinguished Professor Emeritus of English, Wimberley, Texas

W.K. "Kip" Stratton's poetry collection *Betrayal Creek* should be required reading for those who resist poetry, don't like it, or claim it to be useless. Stratton will make you like poetry if you don't. This is not "pretty poetry writing" that scares you away. Stratton finds the simplest, most direct way to express how the simple and unnoticed in our lives have dramatic resonance on what we do with our lives.

These lyrical poems, whether read in chronological order or randomly, have a second person narrator who has just lost a long-term relationship. The use of *you* makes readers recall their own losses. And his investigation into the simplest moments, incidences, and objects in his life makes readers ponder their own bits and pieces of emotionally loaded imagery.

The poems are the narrator's frozen moments as he experiences something familiar. And he finds new relevance in that familiarity: almost always hope mixed with despair. A never-popular restaurant that you like because you felt comfortable in it reveals that it "is everything you are/And everything you ever will be." "She hates boxing, Peckinpah/ Old cowboy movies, and rodeo," so you realize that "You are an ordinary man/With spurs and a saddle-scarred soul."

Eighteen-wheelers, south Texas brush country (where "nothing is painless"), western Oklahoma landscape, South Austin, boxing gyms, old Western movies have hints and reminders and advice. Stratton tells you that at a certain age you have the memories, associations, and interests that condemn you into being you. But if you ponder them, they just might indistinctly whisper a way to survive.

—Jim Sanderson, author of *Nothing to Lose* and *Hill Country Property*

It's not often that a poet dives with such abandon and in such a prolonged way into his own life circumstances as W.K. Stratton does in *Betrayal Creek*. Full of deep-seated disappointment, restlessness, and longing, the poems gain momentum as the poet moves from anger and frustration to understanding and reconciliation with the self.

—Jan Seale, Texas Poet Laureate 2012 and author of *A Lifetime of Words*

W.K. Stratton is an impressively gifted poet with a razor's edge voice. His *Betrayal Creek* offers brutal beauty, late wisdom barely wrenched from deep-soul, that spirit place we never know we have until it's almost too late. The poems are often triggered by sensibility differences between a man and a woman, and the impossibility of bridging them, no matter the sweet vows, no matter how much love or sex. Anticipate a Kirk Douglas Western as prelude to a poet's life, plus Spanish lessons, boxing, Berryman's *Dream Songs*, way too much to drink, and a binge of Dennis Hopper, *The Last Movie*. There's lost love and questionable gain, like a soundtrack of Neil Young, Terry Allen, Lukas Nelson, Los Lobos, and Dave Alvin lamentation songs. Stratton writes, "Dying is a shoulder shrug. Buzzard bait is fine destiny." Yet Stratton's poems offer a kind of salvation, a hope for tomorrow, and he concludes his poetry road trip with a decent manner of self-awareness. Emilio "El Indio" Fernandez is somewhere close and the shade of Sam Peckinpah offers benediction, comprehension, and approval of this book, for W.K Stratton is an important poet of the contemporary West.

—Red Shuttleworth, three-time winner of the Spur Award for Poetry and author of *Western Settings*